CHRISTMAS FAVORITES
FOR OCARINA

ISBN 978-1-5400-2922-5

HAL•LEONARD®

Visit Hal Leonard Online at
www.halleonard.com

Contact Us:
Hal Leonard
7777 West Bluemound Road
Milwaukee, WI 53213
Email: info@halleonard.com

In Europe contact:
Hal Leonard Europe Limited
Distribution Centre, Newmarket Road
Bury St Edmunds, Suffolk, IP33 3YB
Email: info@halleonardeurope.com

In Australia contact:
Hal Leonard Australia Pty. Ltd.
4 Lentara Court
Cheltenham, Victoria, 3192 Australia
Email: info@halleonard.com.au

CONTENTS

BLUE CHRISTMAS

Words and Music by BILLY HAYES
and JAY JOHNSON

With expression

I'll have a blue Christ-mas with-out you. _____ I'll be so

blue think-ing a-bout you. _____ Dec-o-

ra-tions of red on a green Christ-mas tree

won't mean a thing if you're not here with me. I'll have a

blue Christ-mas, that's cer-tain. _____ And when that

blue heart-ache starts hurt-in', _____ you'll be

do-in' al-right, with your Christ-mas of white, but

I'll have a blue, blue Christ-mas. _____

THE CHIPMUNK SONG

Words and Music by
ROSS BAGDASARIAN

THE CHRISTMAS SONG
(Chestnuts Roasting on an Open Fire)

Music and Lyric by MEL TORMÉ
and ROBERT WELLS

CHRISTMAS TIME IS HERE
from A CHARLIE BROWN CHRISTMAS

Words by LEE MENDELSON
Music by VINCE GUARALDI

DO YOU HEAR WHAT I HEAR

Words and Music by NOEL REGNEY
and GLORIA SHAYNE

FELIZ NAVIDAD

Music and Lyrics by
JOSÉ FELICIANO

Moderately

Fe - liz Na - vi - dad. _____ Fe - liz Na - vi - dad. _____ Fe - liz Na - vi -

dad. Pros - pe - ro a - ño y fe - li - ci - dad. _____ Fe - liz Na - vi -

1.

2.

_____ I want to wish you a Mer - ry Christ - mas, with lots of pres - ents to

make you hap - py. I want to wish you a Mer - ry Christ - mas from the bot - tom of my

heart. _____ I want to wish you a Mer - ry Christ - mas, with mis - tle - toe and _

lots of cheer. _ With lots of laugh - ter through - out the years from the bot - tom of my

heart. _____ Fe - liz Na - vi - dad. _____ Fe - liz Na - vi - dad.

_____ Fe - liz Na - vi - dad. Pros - pe - ro a - ño y fe - li - ci - dad. _____

FROSTY THE SNOW MAN

Words and Music by STEVE NELSON
and JACK ROLLINS

HAVE YOURSELF A MERRY LITTLE CHRISTMAS

from MEET ME IN ST. LOUIS

Words and Music by HUGH MARTIN
and RALPH BLANE

HERE COMES SANTA CLAUS
(Right Down Santa Claus Lane)

Words and Music by GENE AUTRY
and OAKLEY HALDEMAN

Moderately, in 2

Here comes San - ta Claus! Here comes San - ta Claus! Right down San - ta Claus

Lane! Vix - en and Blitz - en and all his rein - deer are

pull - ing on the rein. Bells are ring - ing, chil - dren sing - ing,

all is mer - ry and bright. Hang your stock - ings and

say your pray'rs, 'cause San - ta Claus comes to - night.

A HOLLY JOLLY CHRISTMAS

Music and Lyrics by
JOHNNY MARKS

(There's No Place Like)
HOME FOR THE HOLIDAYS

Words and Music by AL STILLMAN
and ROBERT ALLEN

Moderately (♩ = 80)

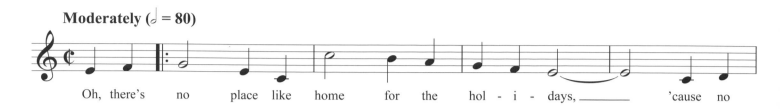

Oh, there's no place like home for the hol-i-days, _____ 'cause no

mat-ter how far a-way you roam, _____ when you

pine for the sun-shine of a friend-ly gaze, _____ for the

hol-i-days you can't beat home sweet home. I met a

man who lives in Ten-nes-see and he was head-in' for Penn-syl-

va-nia and some home-made pump-kin pie. From Penn-syl-

15

va - nia folks are trav - 'lin' down to Dix - ie's sun - ny shores; from At -

lan - tic to Pa - cif - ic, gee, the traf - fic is ter - rif - ic. Oh, there's

no place like home for the hol - i - days, _____ 'cause no

mat - ter how far a - way you roam, _____ if you

want to be hap - py in a mil - lion ways, _____ for the

1.

hol - i - days you can't beat home, sweet home. _____ Oh, there's

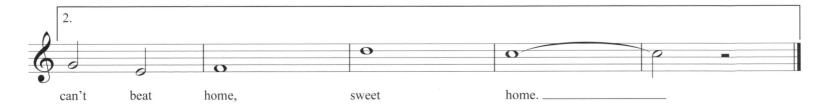

2.

can't beat home, sweet home. _____

I'LL BE HOME FOR CHRISTMAS

Words and Music by KIM GANNON
and WALTER KENT

Slowly

I'll be home for Christ - mas, _____

you can plan on me. _____ Please have

snow and mis - tle - toe and pres - ents

on the tree. _____ Christ - mas Eve will

find me _____ where the love - light

gleams. _____ I'll be home for Christ -

mas, if on - ly in my dreams. _____

IT'S BEGINNING TO LOOK LIKE CHRISTMAS

By MEREDITH WILLSON

LET IT SNOW! LET IT SNOW! LET IT SNOW!

Words by SAMMY CAHN
Music by JULE STYNE

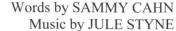

Oh the weath-er out-side is fright-ful, but the fire is so de-
does-n't show signs of stop-ping, and I brought some corn for
fi-re is slow-ly dy-ing, and my dear, we're still good-

light-ful. And since we've no place to go,
pop-ping. The lights are turned way down low,
bye-ing. But as long as you love me so,

let it

To Coda

1.
snow! Let it snow! Let it snow! It

2.
snow! When we

fi-nal-ly kiss good night how I'll hate go-ing out in the

storm! But if you'll real-ly hold me tight

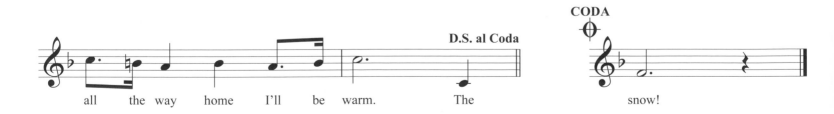

D.S. al Coda

CODA

all the way home I'll be warm. The

snow!

ROCKIN' AROUND THE CHRISTMAS TREE

Music and Lyrics by
JOHNNY MARKS

THE LITTLE DRUMMER BOY

Words and Music by HARRY SIMEONE,
HENRY ONORATI and KATHERINE DAVIS

Moderately

Come, they told me, pa rum pum pum pum, _____
Ba - by Je - su, pa rum pum pum pum, _____

our new-born King to see, pa rum pum pum pum. _____
I am a poor boy, too, pa rum pum pum pum. _____

Our fin - est gifts we bring, pa rum pum pum pum, _____
I have no gift to bring, pa rum pum pum pum, _____

to lay be - fore the King, pa rum pum pum pum, rum pum pum pum,
that's fit to give our King, pa rum pum pum pum, rum pum pum pum,

rum pum pum pum. _____ So to hon - or Him, pa
rum pum pum pum. _____ Shall I play for you, pa

rum pum pum pum, _____   when we come. _____
rum pum pum pum, _____   on __ my   drum? __

_____   Mar - y   nod - ded, pa   rum pum pum   pum. _____

The   ox and lamb kept time, pa   rum pum pum   pum. _____

I   played my   drum for Him, pa   rum pum pum   pum. _____

I   played my   best for Him, pa   rum pum pum pum,   rum pum pum pum,

rum pum pum   pum. _____   Then   He smiled at me, pa

rum pum pum   pum, _____   me and my   drum. _____

THE MOST WONDERFUL TIME OF THE YEAR

Words and Music by EDDIE POLA
and GEORGE WYLE

Brightly, in one

It's the most won - der - ful time _____ of the year, _____
hap - hap - pi - est sea - son of all, _____

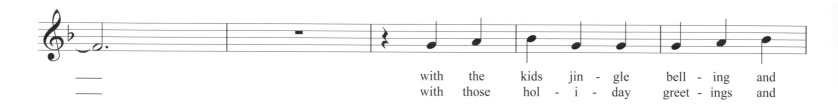

_____ with the kids jin - gle bell - ing and
_____ with those hol - i - day greet - ings and

ev - 'ry - one tell - ing you, "Be of good cheer." _____
gay hap - py meet - ings, when friends come to call. _____

1.

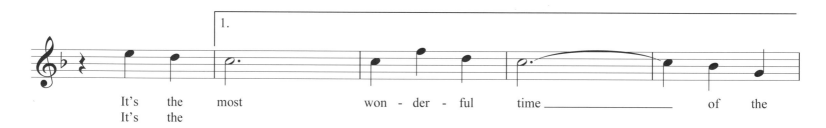

It's the most won - der - ful time _____ of the
It's the

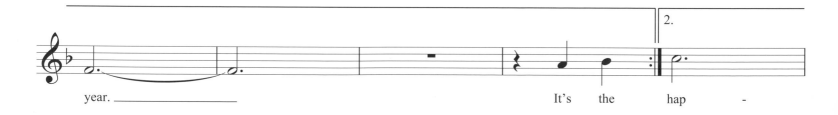

2.

year. _____ It's the hap -

hap - pi - est sea - son of all. _____

RUDOLPH THE RED-NOSED REINDEER

Music and Lyrics by
JOHNNY MARKS

SILVER BELLS

from the Paramount Picture THE LEMON DROP KID

Words and Music by JAY LIVINGSTON
and RAY EVANS

SOMEWHERE IN MY MEMORY

from the Twentieth Century Fox Motion Picture HOME ALONE

Words by LESLIE BRICUSSE
Music by JOHN WILLIAMS

Gently and with simplicity

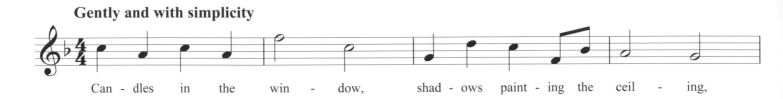

Can - dles in the win - dow, shad - ows paint - ing the ceil - ing,

gaz - ing at the fire glow, feel - ing that "gin - ger - bread" feel - ing.

Pre - cious mo - ments, spe - cial peo - ple, hap - py fac - es I can see.

Some - where in my mem - 'ry, Christ - mas joys all a - round me,

liv - ing in my mem - 'ry, all of the mu - sic, all of the mag - ic,

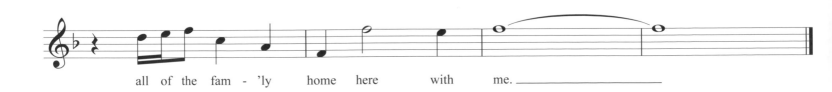

all of the fam - 'ly home here with me.

WE NEED A LITTLE CHRISTMAS

from MAME

Music and Lyric by
JERRY HERMAN

WINTER WONDERLAND

Words by DICK SMITH
Music by FELIX BERNARD

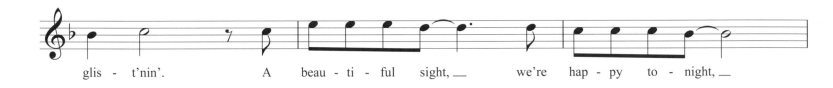

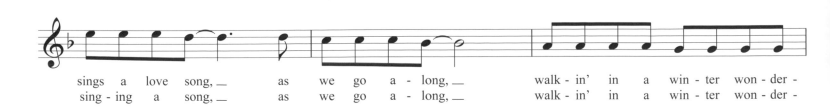

land!   In the mead - ow we can build a snow - man,
land!   In the mead - ow we can build a snow - man,

then pre - tend that he is Par - son Brown.   He'll say, "Are you mar - ried?" We'll say,
and pre - tend that he's a cir - cus clown.   We'll have lots of fun with Mis - ter

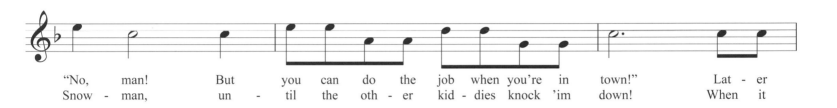

"No, man! But you can do the job when you're in town!" Lat - er
Snow - man, un - til the oth - er kid - dies knock 'im down! When it

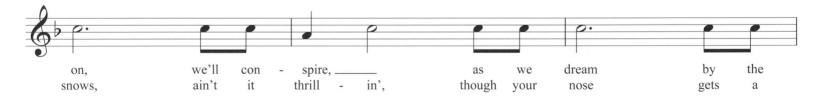

on, we'll con - spire, _____ as we dream   by the
snows, ain't it thrill - in', though your nose   gets a

fire, _____ to face un - a - fraid, __ the plans that we made, __ }
chill - in'? We'll frol - ic and play __ the Es - ki - mo way, __ }

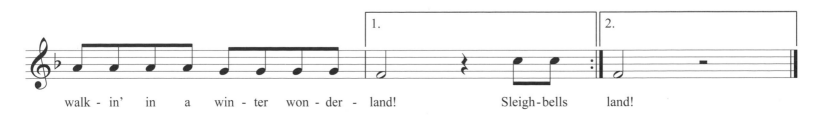

walk - in' in a win - ter won - der - land!   1. Sleigh - bells   2. land!

WHITE CHRISTMAS

from the Motion Picture Irving Berlin's HOLIDAY INN

Words and Music by
IRVING BERLIN

12-Hole Ocarina Fingering Chart

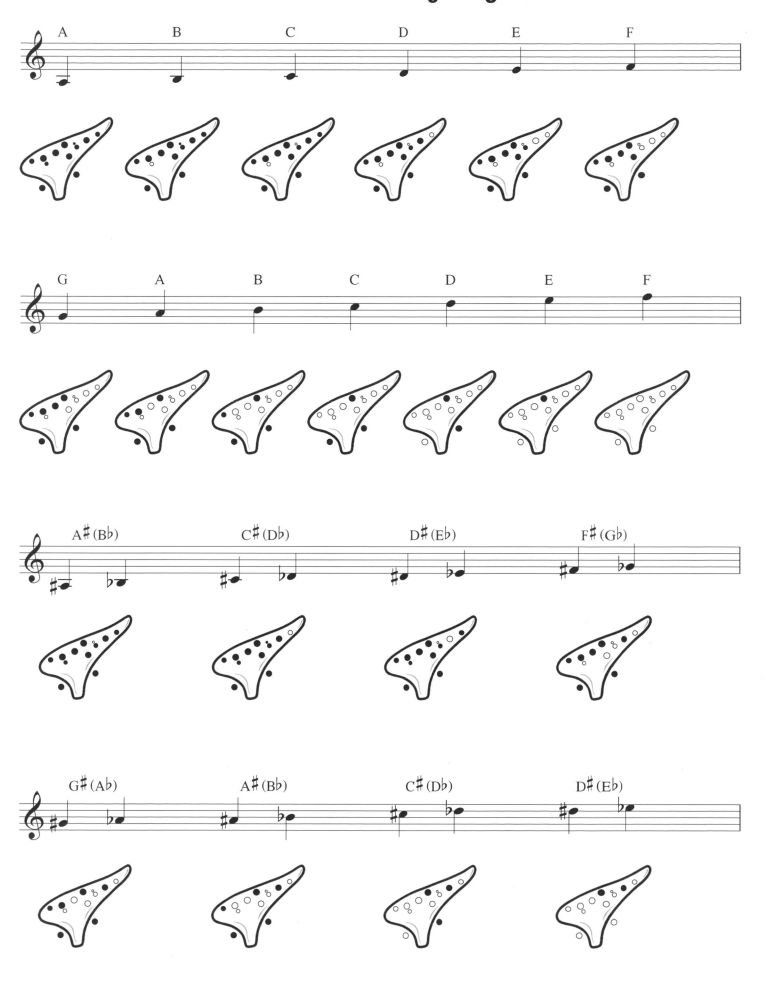

MORE GREAT OCARINA PUBLICATIONS

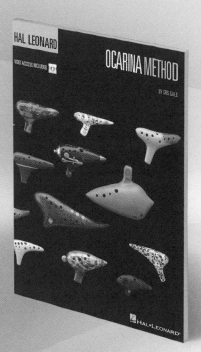

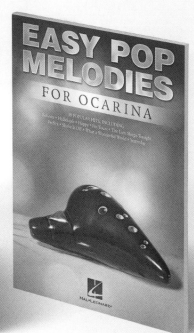
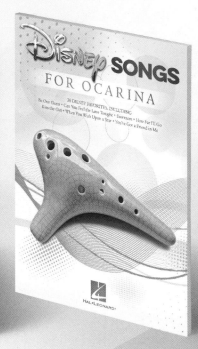

Hal Leonard Ocarina Method
by Cris Gale

The Hal Leonard Ocarina Method is a comprehensive, easy-to-use beginner's guide, designed for anyone just learning to play the ocarina. Inside you'll find loads of techniques, tips and fun songs to learn and play. The accompanying online video, featuring author Cris Gale, provides further instruction as well as demonstrations of the music in the book. Topics covered include: a history of the ocarina • types of ocarinas • breathing and articulation • note names and key signatures • meter signatures and rhythmic notation • fingering charts • many classic folksongs • and more.

00146676   Book/Online Video $12.99

Folk Songs for Ocarina
Arranged for 10-, 11-, and 12-hole ocarinas.

All the Pretty Little Horses • Alouette • Amazing Grace • Annie Laurie • Auld Lang Syne • Aura Lee • The Banana Boat Song • The Blue Bells of Scotland • Danny Boy • Follow the Drinkin' Gourd • Frere Jacques (Are You Sleeping?) • Greensleeves • Hava Nagila (Let's Be Happy) • Home on the Range • Hush, Little Baby • Joshua (Fit the Battle of Jericho) • Kumbaya • La Cucaracha • Little Brown Jug • Loch Lomond • My Bonnie Lies over the Ocean • My Old Kentucky Home • My Wild Irish Rose • Oh! Susanna • Old Dan Tucker • Sakura (Cherry Blossoms) • Scarborough Fair • Shenandoah • Simple Gifts • Skip to My Lou • Sometimes I Feel like a Motherless Child • Swing Low, Sweet Chariot • There Is a Balm in Gilead • This Little Light of Mine • Twinkle, Twinkle Little Star • Volga Boatman Song • Were You There? • When Johnny Comes Marching Home • When the Saints Go Marching In • Yankee Doodle • The Yellow Rose of Texas.

00276000... $9.99

Easy Pop Melodies for Ocarina
Arranged for 10-, 11-, and 12-hole ocarinas.

Believer • Candle in the Wind • City of Stars • Clocks • Edelweiss • Every Breath You Take • (Everything I Do) I Do It for You • Hallelujah • Happy • Hey, Soul Sister • I'm Yours • Let It Be • Let It Go • The Lion Sleeps Tonight • Morning Has Broken • My Girl • My Heart Will Go on (Love Theme from *Titanic*) • Perfect • Roar • Rolling in the Deep • Say Something • Shake It Off • Some Nights • The Sound of Silence • Stay with Me • Sweet Caroline • Uptown Girl • What a Wonderful World • Yesterday • You've Got a Friend.

00275999 .... $9.99

Disney Songs for Ocarina
Arranged for 10-, 11-, and 12-hole ocarinas.

Be Our Guest • Bibbidi-Bobbidi-Boo (The Magic Song) • Can You Feel the Love Tonight • Chim Chim Cher-ee • Colors of the Wind • Do You Want to Build a Snowman? • Evermore • For the First Time in Forever • Hakuna Matata • He's a Pirate • How Does a Moment Last Forever • How Far I'll Go • I Just Can't Wait to Be King • In Summer • Kiss the Girl • Lava • Mickey Mouse March • Seize the Day • Supercalifragilisticexpialidocious • That's How You Know • When You Wish Upon a Star • Whistle While You Work • Who's Afraid of the Big Bad Wolf? • A Whole New World • Winnie the Poo • Yo Ho (A Pirate's Life for Me) • You Can Fly! You Can Fly! You Can Fly! • You're Welcome • You've Got a Friend in Me • Zip-A-Dee-Doo-Dah.

00275998 .... $9.99

HAL•LEONARD®
WWW.HALLEONARD.COM

0318